Preface

The following question bank is all about conceptual understanding. Go through all the questions and try to understand what the question is asking about. Most of the times the aspirants know the material but failed to understand the concept or question. That's why they face failure. Candidates must emphasize in these lines. Try to solve as many questions as they can in order to have deep understanding of the CFA material.

First read the question and understand it. After that read the given options and select the most appropriate option. After selection of the answer, read the answer, given after each question. The answers are given just after each question so the reader feel comfortable and he does not need to go down in search of the answer and the reason of the answer.

Question1: *Board of directors is most likely a*

a. Representative of senior management
b. Representative of Creditors and senior management
c. Representative of shareholders

Answer: The board of directors is the representative of shareholders of the company and exists to protect their interests.

Question 2: Which stakeholder least likely wants the company to undertake riskier projects?
a. Management team
b. Supplier of the firm
c. Creditor

Answer: The correct option is 'c'. The creditor wants the firm to be stable whether the shareholders might want riskier projects to have better expected returns. The management team usually avoids risk but they can also take risk. The supplier is also like the creditor. But the creditor least likely wants the risk

Question 3: Which of the following is least likely a "component of Stakeholder management mechanism?"

a. Legal mechanism

b. Contractual infrastructure

c. Shareholder activism

Answer: All others are component of Stakeholder management except Shareholder activism so answer is 'c'.

Question 4: The typical purposes of extraordinary meetings may include

a. Acquisitions, mergers and presentation of the audited financial statements

b. The presentation about annual growth reports and material change in corporate governance of the company.

c. Acquisitions, mergers and material change in corporate governance

Answer: The answer is 'c'. The typical purposes of extraordinary meetings may include acquisitions, mergers and material change in corporate governance not the presentation of the audited financial statements or the presentation about annual growth reports.

Question 5: Which of the board of director committee ensures that the board of directors is well balanced?

a. Audit committee

b. Governance committee

c. Nomination committee

Answer: The nomination committee nominates the qualified members and ensures that the board of directors is well balanced.

Question6: In a proxy fight

a. Shareholders are persuaded to vote for a control seeking group

b. Shareholders sell their interests directly to a control seeking group.

c. Shareholders try to acquire another company without the consent of management.

Answer: The correct answer is 'a'. 'b' is tender offer and 'c' is hostile takeover.

Question7: Which of the following is *least likely* a result of poor corporate governance structure?

a. Failure of the corporation

b. Shareholders may benefit at cost of customers

c. Operating performance may improve

Answer: The answer is 'c'. because it's the result of good corporate governance not the poor governance.

Question 8: In ESG implementation a negative screening include

a. Only include those companies who have good ESG related principles

b. Exclude some sectors or companies involved in child labor

c. Only include those companies who have highest ESG score in the industry

Answer: In negative screening we exclude some sectors or companies from our

investment considerations. These excluded
companies can involve in issues like increase in
pollution, contaminating water, child labor,
gender inequality bribery, corruption etc. so
the answer is 'b'.

Question 9: Which of the following is most likely a capital project?

    a.   Modernization project
    b.   Launching a new product/service
    c.   Expansion project
    d.   B,c and d.

Answer: All projects from b to c are capital project because their lifespan is more than a year. Modernizing projects does not typically last over a year.

Question 10: What is the first step in capital budgeting process?

a. Idea generating

b. Analyze individual proposals

c. Plan capital budget

Answer: The idea generating is the first step in capital budgeting process.

Question11: In capital budgeting process what is most likely meaning of Plan capital budget?

a.   Generating good ideas is the first and important step.

b.   B. Gather maximum information about each idea

c.   C. Prioritize and organize all those projects who are within firm`s strategies.

Answer: 'c' is the right answer. Point 'a' and 'b' are Idea generating and Analyze individual proposals respectively.

Question 12: Which of the following statement is least likely true?

a. Decisions on capital budgeting are based on cash flows and not only accounting concepts like net income

b. Timings of cash flows are very important. The managers should take good care to forecast the timings of each cash flow.

c. Cash flows are not based on opportunity costs:

Answer: 'c' is the answer. Cash flows are based on opportunity cost. This is the basic principle of capital budgeting. Both 'a' and 'b' are true.

Question13: Which of the following statement is most likely true?

a. Sunk cost is the cost which is already made and cannot be recovered.
b. Sunk cost is the cash flows if we have undertaken a project.
c. Sunk cost is the effect of investment on other projects' cash flows of the same firm

Answer: Sunk cost is the cost which is already made and cannot be recovered, so 'a' is the answer.

Question 14: Which of the following is true for project sequencing?

a. The manager can choose project A or B or both
b. The manager can Chose either project A or B but not both.
c. The projects A and B must be arranged in a manner so that investment in one project can create future investing opportunity in other project

Answer: 'c' is the answer as the name sequencing suggests. Point 'a' and 'b' are _Independent projects and_ mutually exclusive projects respectively.

Question 15: When discount rate used in NPV is equal to IRR which of the following statement is true?

a. NPV profile crosses X –axis
b. NPV profile crosses Y-axls
c. NPV profile is horizontal but above the X axis

Answer: When NPV crosses X axis it means the discount rate is used to calculate NPV is equal to IRR. So the answer is 'a'.

Question 16: Project A has higher IRR but lower NPV. Project B has lower IRR but higher NPV. Which project should be selected?

a. Project A
b. Project B
c. None of the above

Answer: When NPV and IRR show different results the NPV is preferred over IRR. So the project with higher NPV is selected.

Question 17: If a company undertakes a project with positive NPV (all other factors remains constant), which of the following statements is true?

a. The market price of Stock of the company will rise by the NPV amount
b. The market price of the company stock would remain neutral
c. There would be a positive effect on stock price in the market.

Answer: The answer is c. A company with a positive NPV project will signal a positive effect in the market. But this affect may not be proportional to the amount of NPV as the market price shows investor's expectations about company`s future.

Question 18: A company has following capital structure. 25% debt, 30% preferred equity and 45% common stock. Marginal cost of debt is 7% (before tax), marginal cost of preferred stock is 8% and marginal cost of common equity is 9%. Its marginal tax rate is 50%. What is the weighted average cost of capital?

a. 6.23%

b.7.23%

c. 8%

Answer:

$WACC = W_d * K_d(1-t) + W_{ps} * K_{ps} + W_{ce} * K_{ce}$

$WACC = (0.25)(0.07)(1-0.50) + (0.30)(0.08) + (0.45)(0.09)$

$WACC = 7.325\%$ the answer is b.

Question 19: The WACC is also called

a. Sunk cost
b. Preliminary expenses
c. Opportunity cost

Answer: WACC is also opportunity cost for the company. Imagine if the company has not raised these funds to finance certain assets, it could have saved this cost

Question 20: Which statement(s) is (are) true?

WACC is also the discount rate for capital budgeting.

If WACC is greater than IRR then the project is viable otherwise not.

a. Only first statement
b. Only second statement
c. Both statements

Answer: Answer is a. WACC is the discount rate to be used in capital budgeting. Second statement is false. For a project to be viable, the IRR must be greater than WACC. Remember the IRR is the rate of return while the WACC is the cost.

Question 21: Which of the following is most likely true?

a. Cost of preferred stock is tax deductible
b. Cost of common equity is tax deductible
c. Cost of debt is tax deductible

Answer: The cost of debt is tax deductible that's why we use Kd(1-t) in WACC.

Preferred equity and common equities are not affected by tax rate as they are not tax deductible. Answer is c.

Question 22: What is the targeted capital structure of ABC Company?

a. The explicitly disclosed "targeted capital structure" by management.
b. Industry average capital structure.
c. Current capital structure of the company.

Answer: The explicitly disclosed targeted capital structure by management is the targeted capital structure of the company. If there is no explicitly disclosed targeted capital structure is available then we can assume either industry average or current capital structure of the company as targeted. So the answer is a.

Question 23: If a company has $10m as debt and $15m as common equity (these are market values) and there is no other information available, what is the targeted capital structure of the company?

a.50% debt 50% Equity

b.60% debt 40% Equity

c.40% debt 60% Equity

Answer: When there is no other information available, we can assume the current capital structure is the targeted capital structure. We just need to calculate the weight of the components of capital.

Wd= 10/(10+15) = 40%.

Wce = 15/(10+15) = 60%.

The answer is c.

Question 24: Which of the following statements is most likely true?

a. Investment opportunity line has negative trend because the marginal cost of capital increases.

b. Investment opportunity line has negative trend because of negative IRR

c. Investment opportunity line has negative trend because every with every new project the IRR decreases.

Answer: when firm involves in launching more and more investment projects, then the every new project usually gives less and less return

(IRR). It is mainly because at first, the firm tries to invest in a project with highest IRR and then second project with second highest IRR and so on. So the investment opportunity schedule line has negative trend. So the answer is c. Both 'a' and 'b' are incorrect because the investment opportunity line is not affected by marginal cost of capital and the IRR is not necessarily to be negative for the investment opportunity line to have negative trend.

Question25: Which of the following statements is true?

a. All points on investment opportunity line are optimal projects a company can undertake.
b. All points on MCC line are optimal projects a company can undertake.
c. All the points on and above the intersection of investment opportunity line and WACC are optimal.

Answer: As long as the IRR is greater than cost of capital the firm is adding value in shareholders` equity. The intersection point of WACC and Investment opportunity line shows the firm should stop investing. There would be losses after this point. So the Answer is c.

Question 26: Company ABC is going to undertake a project with initial investment of $100m. the project is expected to have positive cash flows of $10 m, $50m and $60m is year 1,2 and 3. The marginal cost of capital is 4%. What is the NPV of that project?

a.$8.18m

b. $9.18m

c.$10.18m

Answer: $$NPV = \frac{Cash\ flow1}{(1+MCC)^1} + \frac{Cash\ flow2}{(1+MCC)^2} + \ldots\ldots$$

$$\frac{Cash\ flow\,'n}{(1+MCC)^n}$$

$$NPV = -100 + \frac{10}{(1+0.04)^1} + \frac{50}{(1+0.04)^2} + \frac{60}{(1+0.04)^3}$$

NPV= $9.18m The Answer is b.

Question 27: If the new project is riskier than firm`s overall risk the discount rate to calculate NPV of that project must be

    a. Greater than MCC
    b. Less than MCC
    c. Equal to MCC

Answer: By using MCC as discount rate we assume that

- The total risk of the firm will remain same during the life of project and
- The risk of new project is same as the firm`s total risk

But in reality risk of a project may differ from the firm`s total risk so we should make some adjustments in discount rate while calculating NPV.

If a project is more risky (than firm`s total risk profile), then the discount rate should be higher than MCC.

Question 28: Yield to maturity is
  a. The total return on a bond if it is held until maturity.
  b. The total return on a bond if it is sold before maturity
  c. The total return on a bond if it is bought and sold in same day.

Answer: The answer is 'a'. It is the definition of YTM.

Question 29: The YTM equates the present value of coupon and principal payments to
  a. The current market value of the bond
  b. The face value of bond
  c. Net present value of bond

Answer: The YTM equates the present value of coupon and principal payments to the

current market value of the bond. The answer
is 'a'.

**Question 30: If the firm`s debt is not
being traded in market or the market is
very illiquid, how we can calculate YTM?**

   a. By taking equity shares of same
      company and calculate its rate of
      return.
   b. By taking preferred shares of same
      company and calculate its rate of
      return
   c. By using a comparable company`s
      comparable debt of same maturity

Answer: If the firm`s debt is not being traded
in market or the market is very illiquid, we can
use debt rating approach to calculate pretax
cost of debt by using other debt issued by the
same company with same maturity. If it is also
not available then we can estimate it by using
a comparable company`s comparable debt of

same maturity. The comparable debt and company can have following characteristics

- Same sized company
- Same industry
- Same business
- Same risk exposure
- Debt with similar risks etc

So the Answer is c.

Question 31: Non-callable preferred stock is the preferred stock which

a. Can be redeemed by the issuer
b. Which cannot be converted into common stocks by the investor
c. Cannot be redeemed by the issuer

Answer: The answer is 'c' as it is the definition of non-callable preferred stock.

Question32: Non-convertible preferred stock is the preferred stock

a. which cannot be converted into common stocks by the investor

b. Which cannot be converted into common stocks by the investor

c. Cannot be redeemed by the issuer

Answer: The answer is 'a' as the name suggests.

Question 33: A company issues non-callable, non-convertible preferred stock priced at $101 with dividend of 4%. What is the cost of preferred stock?

a.3%

b.4.8%

c.3.98%

Answer: Cost of preferred stock can be calculated as

Kps = Dps/Pps

=4/101

=3.96%. Sothe answer is 'c'.

Question 34: Which of the following statement is true?

a. Cost of preferred stock is tax deductible

b. Cost of debt is not tax deductible

c. Cost of preferred stock is not tax deductible

Answer: The answer is 'c' as the cost of preferred stock is not tax deductible. Only cost of debt is tax deductible.

Question 35: Consider a firm is being traded in a market with market rate of return of 7 percent. The firm's beta is 1.5 (The risk is more than market). The risk-free rate is 3%. What is cost of equity of firm using CAPM?

a. 8%

b. 9%

c. 10%

Answer:

$E(Ri) = Rf + \beta i[E(Rm) - Rf]$

$= 0.03 + 1.5(0.07 - 0.03) = 9\%$ Answer is b.

Question36: Which of the following statements is most likely true?

a. Dividend discount model considers 'Risk free rate of return', 'expected market rate of return' and 'Beta of investment'.

b. Dividend discount model consider the current market price and expected future dividends of a security.

c. With dividend discount model the cost of equity must be cost of bond plus risk premium for the common equity.

Answer: Dividend discount model consider the current market price and expected future dividends of a security. The options 'a' and 'c' are true in case of CAPM and Bond-yield plus risk-premium approach respectively.

Question 37: A company's shares are being traded at $10. Company's next expected dividend is $2. Considering a constant growth of 4% what is the cost of equity using dividend discount model?

a. 20%

b. 22%

c. 24%

Answer: Cost of equity formula for DDM

$K_{ce} = D_1/(P_o) + g$

$K_{ce} = 2/10 + 0.04 = 24\%$ the Answer is 'c'.

Question 38: There is no active market for the shares of ABC Company. The same company has a bond with YTM of 5% and investors want 3 percent risk premium for the equity. What is the cost of equity for ABC Company?

a. 2%

b. 5%

c.8%

Answer: As there is no active market for the equity we can use Bond-yield plus risk-premium approach.

$K_{ce} = K_d + $ risk premium

Cost of equity = 5% + 3% = 8% the answer is c.

Question 39: Which of the following statements is most likely true?

a. In CAPM model we use beta for systematic risk of a security in comparison to market risk.
b. If the company is not being traded in the market or there is no active market for that company is available, we can estimate beta using CAPM model.
c. if the company is not being traded in the market or there is no active market for that company is available then we use a method called PURE PLAY to estimate beta

Answer: In CAPM model we use beta for systematic risk of a security in comparison to market risk.

Cost of capital using CAPM model =
$$E(Ri)=Rf+\beta i[E(Rm)-Rf]$$

For a publically traded company the calculation of beta and cost of equity is easy.

But if the company is not being traded in the market or there is no active market for that company is available then we use a method called PURE PLAY to estimate beta. The answer is 'c'.

Question 40: Which of the following statements is true?

   a. The use of CAPM is not a good estimate cost of equity in underdeveloped countries

   b. The use of CAPM is a good estimate cost of equity in underdeveloped countries.

   c. CAPM model is not a good estimate of cost of equity in any market.

Answer: The use of CAPM to estimate cost of equity is tricky in underdeveloped and developing countries because the beta does not capture country risk. A country risk premium is added in market risk to come up with a better estimate of cost of equity. The answer is 'a'.

Question 41: Let's say Country X's 5-year government bond yield is 8%. A USA treasury bond with same maturity has 4% yield. Annualized SD of equity index in X country is 40% and the annualized standard deviation of country X's 5-year government bond denominated in USD is 21%. Calculate country X's risk premium?

a. 8.32%

b. 9.62%

c. 7.61%

Answer: *Sovereign yield spread = 8%-4% =4%*

$$CRP = \text{Sovereign yield spread} \times \frac{\text{Annualized SD of equity index in developing country}}{\text{Annualized SD of sovereign bond market in terms of developed market currency}}$$

4% x(40%/21%) = 7.61%. The answer is 'c'.

After adding CRP the CAPM would be like this

Cost of equity using CAPM model =

E(Ri)=Rf+βi[E(Rm)−Rf + CRP]

Question 42: Marginal cost of capital (MCC) has upward trend because;

a. If a firm raise more debt capital the cost of equity also increases because the firm is getting more risky and the investors want higher required rate of return to invest in equity capital
b. Not because of debt covenants (the restrictions imposed by lenders on the borrower.
c. Because of IRR

Answer: If a firm raise more debt capital the cost of equity also increases because the firm is getting more risky and the investors want higher required rate of return to invest in equity capital. MCC also has upward trend because of debt covenants. IRR does not have to do anything with upward trend of MCC.

Question 43: Which of the following statements is most likely true?

a. MCC is not a smooth upward graph, but is a step up graph
b. MCC is a smooth upward graph
c. MCC is parallel to X axis.

Answer: In reality, the MCC is not a smooth upward graph, but is a step up graph and every start of the step is called break point. The answer is 'a'.

Question 44: Which of the following statements is most likely true with respect to Floatation cost?

a. It is the cost which is already made and cannot be recovered.
b. The cost of best alternative foregone
c. Cost in the process of raising additional capital

Answer: The answer is 'c'. Companies have to bear some cost in the process of raising additional capital. These costs are called

flotation costs. The amount of flotation cost
depends on the amount of and types of capital
being raised.

For example the flotation cost in case of debt
and preferred equity is negligible. In case of
common equity, the flotation cost could be
very high (usually 2% to 7% of capital being
raised). Usually a major portion of flotation
cost comprise of investment bank`s fee (the
investment bank who helps the company to
raise

capital).

'a' is sunk cost While 'b' is the opportunity
cost.

**Question 45: Which of the following
statements is most likely true?**

    a. Flotation cost in case of debt is higher
       than preferred and common equity.

    b. Flotation cost in case of preferred stock
       is higher than debt and common equity.

    c. Flotation cost in case of common equity
       is higher than preferred and debt.

Answer: Flotation cost in case of debt and preferred equity is negligible. In case of common equity, the flotation cost could be very high (usually 2% to 7% of capital being raised). Usually a major portion of flotation cost comprise of investment bank`s fee (the investment bank who helps the company to raise capital). So the answer is 'c'.

Question 46: The correct treatment of flotation cost is

    a. It should be added in cost of equity.

    b. It should be added into first time outflow of the project.

    c. Never add flotation cost in any other cost.

Answer: As the floating cost is one time outflow, it should be added into first time outflow of the project. If the flotation cost is would be added in cost of equity the WACC increases and later while evaluating the project, we would be discounting the project at higher discount rate. With this treatment we will come up with wrong estimates of NPV of the project. So the correct answer is 'b'.

Question 47: Which of the following statements is true?

a. Rent is included in operating leverage
b. Borrowed money is included in operating leverage
c. Uncertainty of sales in future is operating leverage.

Answer: The answer is 'a'. Rent and depreciations etc are included in operating leverage. Use of borrowed money is financial leverage while uncertainty of sales is sales risk.

Question 48: Which of the following statements is *least likely* true?

a. Highly leveraged company`s profits and losses can be magnified.
b. Highly leveraged company`s risk characteristics also increases.

c. Leverage does not have any effect on risk or returns.

Answer: Highly leveraged company has more returns as well as risks. So the statements 'a' and 'b' are true while statement 'c' is not true or least likely true. (c is the answer).

Question 49: Business risk has two components;

a. Sales risk and financial risk

b. Financial risk and operating risk

c. Operating risk and sales risk

Answer: Business risk of a firm consists of sales risk and operating risk. It arises from the financial leverage. So the answer is 'c'.

Question 50: If a company has to pay higher amount of interest, which type of risk the company is most likely facing?

a. Operating risk

b. Business risk

c. Financial risk

Answer: Financial risk arises from the financial leverage. If a company has more debt (so it has to pay fixed interest rate) relative to common equity in capital structure, more the financial risk the company has. So the answer is 'c'.

Question 51: Which of the following statements is most likely true?

a. Degree of operating leverage is the percentage change in operating income due to percentage change in sales.
b. Degree of financial leverage (DFL) is the combination of DOL and DFL.
c. Degree of total leverage (DTL) is used to measure the financial risk.

Answer: Degree of operating leverage is the percentage change in operating income due to percentage change in sales. It measures the sensitivity of EBIT towards sales. It can also be defined as "measurement of firm`s operating risk". The answer is 'a'. Degree of financial leverage (DFL) is used to measure the financial risk. Degree of total leverage is the combination of DOL and DFL.

Question 52: EBIT is used as numerator in

    a. FRL

    b. DTL

    c. DOL

Answer: The Earning before interest and tax is used as numerator in DOL. In DFL and DTL, the EBIT is used in denominator.

Question 53: A company is selling each pair of shoes at $10. It is facing $3000 as fixed cost while $2 is per unit variable cost. If the firm is selling 2000 units of shoes, what is the DOL?

    a. 1.23

    b. 1.3

    c. 1.32

    Answer:

$$DOL = \frac{PQ - VQ}{PQ - VQ - F}$$

$$DOL = \frac{(10)\,(2000) - (2)\,(2000)}{(10)\,(2000) - (2)\,(2000) - 3000}$$

DOL= 1.23 the answer is 'a'

Question 54: If a company has 3 % DOL, What does this means?

   a. It means if the sales changes (increase or decrease) by 3% then, our operating income will change by 1%.

   b. It means if there is a change of 1% in EBIT, then the net income will change by 3%.

   c. It means if the sales changes (increase or decrease) by 1% then, our operating income will change by 3%.

Answer: The answer is 'c'. It is the percentage change in operating income due to percentage change in sales. It measures the sensitivity of EBIT towards sales. It can also be defined as "measurement of firm`s operating risk".

Question 55: The percentage change in net income due to percentage change in operating income is called?

    a. DOL

    b. DFL

    c. DTL

Answer: The answer is 'b' as the DFL (degree of financial leverage) means percentage change in net income due to percentage change in operating income.

Question 56: A company's total revenues are $3000 while cost of goods sold is $1400. The company is paying $500 as fixed cost while it has a debt of $20000 at 4%. In the absence of any other information, what is the company's degree of financial leverage?

a.3.67

b. 2.67

c. 1.67

Answer:

$$DFL = \frac{PQ - QV - F}{PQ - VQ - F - I}$$

Total revenues are PQ,

And we can use cost of goods sold as an estimate for QV as the COGS are mainly consist of total variable cost (VQ). The interest amount is $800 (20000 x 4%). Now put these values in the above formula

$$DFL = \frac{3000 - 1400 - 500}{3000 - 1400 - 500 - 800}$$

DFL = 3.67 the answer is 'a'.

Question 57: A company's DFL is 1.3 and DOL is 2. Its degree of total leverage is closest to?

a. 1.3

b.2

c.2.6

Answer: DTL = DFL x DOL = 1.3 x 2 = 2.6 the answer is c.

Question 58: Degree to total leverage measures

a. The sensitivity of net income towards sales.

b. The financial risk

c. Sensitivity of net income towards operating income.

Answer: Degree of total leverage is the combination of DOL and DFL.

DTL = DOL x DFL

$$DTL = \frac{\%\Delta\ EBIT}{\%\ \Delta\ in\ sales} \ x\ \frac{\%\Delta\ net\ income}{\%\ \Delta\ EBIT}$$

Or

$$DTL = \frac{\%\Delta\ Net\ income}{\%\ \Delta\ in\ sales}$$

The correct answer is 'a'.

Question 59: Which of the following statement is most likely true?

a. Use of debt magnifies the profits on equity (ROE)

b. Use of debt magnifies the profits and losses on equity.

c. Use of debt has no effect on ROE

Answer: Use of debt magnifies the profits and losses on equity not just profits. Return on equity (ROE) = Net income / Shares holders` equity

When we have some assets financed by debt capital, it will reduce the net income by interest paid. But when we calculate the ROE, we do not include debt in divider. So we come up with higher ROE. So in case of profit, ROE is magnified while in case of losses the ROE also magnifies the losses. The correct answer is 'b'.

Question 60: Which of the following statements is least likely true?

a. Break even means a situation of no profit no loss.

b. Break even means where Total revenues are equal to total cost.

c. Break even means the amount of capital where cost of capital changes.

Answer: Breakeven point is a situation of no profit no loss is called breakeven. The quantity at which there is no profit and no loss is called breakeven quantity. (Total revenues = total cost). Amount of capital where cost of capital changes is called break point of cost of capital. So the 'c' statement is least likely true.

Question 61: The total of fixed and financial cost of a company is $10000. The price per unit is $10 while the variable cost is $5/ unit. What is the breakeven point for this company?

a. 1000 units

b.2000 units

c.3000 units

Answer:

$$QBE = \frac{(F + I)}{P - v}$$

$$QBE = \frac{10000}{10-5} = 2000 \text{ units. The answer us 'b'.}$$

Question 62: Contribution margin in breakeven is

   a. TR = TC

   b. P −v

   c. P +V

Answer: P-V" is the contribution margin per unit because it helps to cover fixed cost. The answer is 'b'.

Question 63: A company ABC has fixed operating cost of $8000 and interest payment of $5000. The contribution margin is 8. The operating breakeven quantity is closest to

a. 375 units

b. 625 units

c. 1000 units

Answer:

$$\text{QoBE} = \dfrac{\dfrac{F}{P - v}}{}$$

$$\text{QoBE} = \dfrac{8000}{8} = 1000 \text{ units the answer is 'c'.}$$

The interest payment has nothing to do with operating breakeven.

Question 64: Operating breakeven means

    a.   The level of sales at which total cost is just equal to total revenues.

    b.   The level of sales at which total cost is equal to total fixed cost

    c.   The level of sales at which the total revenues are just equal to operating cost".

Answer: As the name suggests, operating breakeven point means "the level of sales at which the total revenues are just equal to operating cost". The correct answer is 'c'.

Question 65: Which of the following statements is least likely true?

a. Companies need liquidity to acquire machinery.
b. Companies need liquidity to pay daily wages.
c. Companies need liquidity to pay to suppliers.

Answer: Companies liquidity to meet short term obligations (like payments of wages and to creditors). So 'a' is least likely true.

Question 66: Which of the following statements is most likely true?

a. Use of primary sources of liquidity does not affect company`s normal course of business.
b. Use of primary sources of liquidity do affect company`s normal course of business.
c. Use of secondary sources of liquidity does not affect company`s normal course of business.

Answer: Use of primary sources of liquidity does not affect company`s normal course of business. The use of secondary sources of liquidity changes the normal course of business. It can change the capital structure of the company and its operations. Use of secondary sources can be a sign of poor management.

Question 67: Account receivables are ---- source of liquidity

   a. Primary
   b. Secondary
   c. Not a source of liquidity

Answer: Balance in bank, Cash received from customers, line of credit from bank etc are primary source of liquidity for a firm.

Question 68: Filing bankruptcy is a ---- source of liquidity

   a. Primary
   b. Secondary

c. Not a source

Answer: Negotiated or re-negotiated debt, Selling current (inventory) and long lived assets and, Filing bankruptcy are some secondary sources of liquidity for the firm.

Question 69: _Drags on liquidity includes_

a. Uncollected receivables and Early payments
b. Reducing and or limiting the credit lines
c. Uncollected receivables and increase in bad debts

Answer: Any factor which reduces the inflows of cash are called drags on liquidity. Uncollected receivables, increase in bad debts, higher discounts on sales, inventory is getting obsolete (because it takes more time to sale) and higher cost of borrowings (tight credit) are "drags on liquidity". So the correct answer is 'c'. 'a' is wrong because early payments are not drags on liquidity rather pulls on liquidity.

Question 70: A firm`s liquidity is measured with the help of

   a. Solvency ratios
   b. Debt ratios
   c. Liquidity ratios

Answer: A firm`s liquidity is measured with the help of liquidity ratios. The correct answer is 'c'.

Question 71: Which of the following is least likely true?

   a. A current ratio of 1 indicates that the company's current assets are equals the dollar value of their current liabilities.
   b. A current ratio of 1 indicates that the company's short-term obligations are just covered
   c. A current ratio of 1 indicates the company is relying on operating profit to meet short term obligations because current assets are not enough.

Answer: A current ratio of one indicates that the company's current assets are equals the dollar value of their current liabilities. So, the short-term obligations are just covered. A ratio less than one means that the company is relying on operating profit to meet short term obligations because current assets are not enough. So least accurate is 'c'.

Question 72: Which of the following statements is most likely true?

a. Current ratio is better estimate of liquidity than quick ratio.
b. Quick ratio is a better estimation of liquidity than current ratio
c. Both ratios produce same results.

Answer: Quick ratio is more realistic approach about our ability to convert certain current assets into cash. Pre-payments for example might be included in the current assets of a company but would be are very difficult to turn into cash. Same is the case with inventory. So, we exclude these two in quick ratio to have more meaningful results.

So the answer is 'b'.

Question 73: The most conservative approach is

a. Current ratio
b. Quick ratio
c. Cash ratio

Answer: With cash ratio we are more conservative about the asset`s ability to meet short-term obligations. We only include most liquid assets. We only include cash and marketable securities the company has right now to pay their short term obligations.

Use the following data for questions 74 to 76.

A company has following assets and liabilities;

Total current assets = $10000

Inventory= $1000

Prepayments = $800

Marketable securities= $5000

Cash balance = $2000

Total current liabilities = $10000

Find

Quick ratio = 10000 – 1000 - 800 = 8200/10000 = 0.82

Quick ratio= 2000 + 5000 = 7000/10000 = 0.7

Question 74: What is the current ratio?

a. 1

b.0.7

c.0.82

Answer: Current ratio = CA/CL = 10000/10000 = 1 the answer is 'a'.

Question 75: What is quick ratio?

a. 1

b.0.7

c.0.82

Answer:

Quick ratio= (Current assets – inventory – pre-payments)/CL

Quick ratio = (10000 – 1000 – 800)/10000 = 8200/10000 = 0.82

Question 76: What is cash ratio?

a. 1

b.0.7

c.0.82

Cash ratio= (Cash balance + marketable securities)/CL = 7000/10000 = 0.7

Cash ratio= 2000 + 5000 = 7000/10000 = 0.7

Question 77: Inventory turnover means?

    a. The average processing period of inventory to turn into sales.
    b. How many times company pays its payables completely
    c. How many times the firm has sold its inventory completely

Answer: Inventory turnover means how many times the firm has sold its inventory completely (at least theoretically).

Question 78: A company's inventory at start of the year is $20000 and increased to $25000 at end of the year. The cost of goods sold is $30000. What is Inventory turnover for this company?

a. 1.33

b. 0.75

c. 1

Answer:

Inventory turnover ratio= Cost of goods sold/ average inventory

Inventory turnover ratio= 30000/ 22500 = 1.33 times

The answer is 'a'.

Question 79: Number of days of inventory tells us?

a. The average processing period of inventory to turn into sales.
b. How many times company pays its payables completely
c. How many times the firm has sold its inventory completely

Answer: Number of days of inventory tells us the average processing period of inventory to turn into sales. The answer is 'a'.

Question 80: Using the data of question 78, what is "number of days inventory?

a.365 days

b. 200 days

c. 274.43 days

Answer:

Number of days of inventory =

$$\frac{365}{\textit{Inventory turnover ratio}}$$

Number of days of inventory = 365/1.33

Number of days of inventory = 274.43 days

The answer is 'c'.

Question 81: Payable turnover ratio tells us

a. The average processing period of inventory to turn into sales.
b. How many times company pays its payables completely
c. How many times the firm has sold its inventory completely

Answer: Payable turnover ratio = purchases/ average payables: It means how many times company pays its payables completely (theoretically).

Question 82: During a financial year a company ABC has total purchases of $20000. The ending balance of payables is $15000. With no other information available what is the company's payable turnover ratio?

a. 0.75 times

b.1 times

c.1.33 times

Answer: With no other information available we can use ending balance of payables instead of average payables.

Payable turnover ratio = purchases/ average payables

Payable turnover ratio = 20000/ 15000

Payable turnover ratio = 1.33 times

The answer is 'c'.

Question 83: Number of days of payables tells us;

a. How many days a firm takes to pay its creditors.

b. How many times company pays its payables completely

c. How many times the firm has sold its inventory completely

Answer: Number of days of payables tells us how many days a firm takes to pay its creditors.

Question 84: A company has payable turnover ratio of 2. What is "number of days of payables"?

a. 182.5 days

b. 100 days

c. 190 days

Answer: Number of days of payables= 365/ payable turnover ratio

Number of days of payables= 365/ 2

Number of days of payables= 182.5 days. The answer is 'a'.

Question 85: _Committed and Uncommitted line of credit_ are classified as

     a. Short term non-banking funding choices

     b. Long term non-banking funding choices

     c. Short term banking funding choices

Answer: The above two are classified as short term banking funding choices available to any company.

Uncommitted line of credit: The bank offers a certain amount but can refuse if the situation changes as there is no formal commitment from bank. _Committed or regular line of credit (Overdraft):_ It is a formal commitment from banks to extend loans (also called overdraft). The banks usually charge fee for such commitment.

Question 86: Commercial papers can be classified as;

     a. Short term non-banking funding choice

     b. Long term non-banking funding choice

     c. Short term banking funding choice

Answer: Commercial papers and non-bank credit institutes can be classified as non-banking short term funding choices for a company.

Question 87: For short term funding requirements, which financing method a company should choose?

    a. Short term funding from bank

    b. Short term non- banking funding

    c. The least costly funding choice

Answer: The Company should choose the method which gives more proceeds and least cost. So the 'c' is correct answer.

Question 88: Which statement is least likely true?

    a. Capital rationing means limiting the funds to a project

    b. Capital rationing is done due to limited resources or due to availability of other more profitable projects.

c. Capital rationing means the projects must be arranged in a manner so that investment on one project can create future investing opportunity in other project

Answer: Capital rationing means limiting the funds to a project. Capital rationing is done due to limited resources or due to availability of other more profitable projects. 'a' and 'b' are true. 'c' is project sequencing so 'c' is least likely true.

Question 89: Two projects A and B are under consideration. Project A has 2 years of payback period. Project B has 1.5 years of payback.

a. Project with higher payback period is better

b. Project with lower payback period is better

c. Payback period has nothing to do while choosing the project.

Answer: Payback period measures how much time it will take to return us original investment so the project with lower payback period is better. So 'b' is the answer.

Question 90:

year	0	1	2	3
Cash flow	-500	100	450	300
Cumulative cash flow	-500	400	50	350

What is the payback period of this project?

a.

b.

c.

Answer:

Payback period=

Full years until recovery year +

$$\frac{un\text{-}recovered\,cost\ at\ the\ begining\ of\ recovered\ year}{Cash\ flow\ during\ recoverd\ year}$$

Payback period $= 1 + \dfrac{100}{450} = 1.223$ years

Question 91: Profitability index is

a. The present value of all future cash flows divided by initial investment.
b. The present value of all future cash flows minus initial investment.
c. Is same just like simple payback period but here we use discounted cash flows.

Answer: Profitability index is the present value of all future cash flows divided by initial investment. PI$= \dfrac{Present\ value\ of\ all\ cash\ flows}{Initial\ investment}$

Question 92: With respect to profitability index which statement is true?

a. If PI<1, undertake the project
b. PI>1, undertake the project
c. PI=1, undertake the project

Answer: If profitability index is greater than 1, it means the project is paying back more than initial investment. It means we should undertake the project (all else being same)

If the profitability index is less than 1 it means the projects inflows are less than initial investments. If the profitability index is just equal to 1 it means the project is just returning our original investment. So we can undertake a project if it's PI is greater than one. So 'b' is the answer.

Question 93: In ESG implementation what is thematic investment?

a. In this method we exclude some sectors or companies from our investment considerations.

b. In this method we only include those companies who have highest ESG score in the industry.

c. In this approach we consider all those companies who are involved specific ESG goals like energy efficiency.

Answer: Thematic investment: In this approach we consider all those companies who are involved specific ESG goals like energy efficiency and climate change. For example companies using water and clean energy sources efficiently.

Question 94: Replacing project may include;

a. Increase in size of the company.
b. Replacing old machinery, plan and equipments
c. Launching new products.

Answer: Replacement projects: These projects can include replacing old machinery, plan and equipments, replacement of machinery etc. so 'b' is the correct answer. 'a' and 'c' are expansion projects and New product projects respectively.

Question 95: Conventional cash flows means

a. Initial outflow and then a series of inflows
b. Initial outflows then inflows and then outflows.
c. Initial inflows and then outflows.

Answer: Conventional cash flows mean Initial outflow and then a series of inflows. 'b' and 'c' are unconventional cash flows.

Replacement projects: These projects can include replacing old machinery, plan and equipments, replacement of machinery etc.

d. **Expansion projects:** Increase in size of the company.

e. **New product:** Launching new products.

f. **Regulatory projects:** The projects required by government or regulatory bodies.

g.

9 7 9 8 6 8 2 8 3 1 0 9 8